I0100861

Ron Ovadia, for ARE Outrigger World

A SPECIAL KIND OF

FAMILY

Illustrated by Penny Weber

HIGHPOINT Life

Copyright © 2022 by ARE Outrigger World

All rights reserved. Published in the United States of America. No part
of this book may be reproduced or transmitted in any form or by any
means, graphic, electronic or mechanical, including photocopying,
recording, taping or by any information storage or retrieval system,
without permission in writing from the publisher.

This edition published by Highpoint Life,
an imprint of Highpoint Executive Publishing.
For information, write to info@highpointpubs.com.

First Edition
ISBN: 979-8-9862590-4-8

Ovadia, Ron
A Special Kind of Family

Illustrated by Penny Weber
Production Assistance: Sarah Clarehart

ISBN: 979-8-9862590-4-8 (Hardcover)
1. Family 2. Mind and Body

Library of Congress Control Number: 2022917026

Manufactured in the United States of America

A Special Kind of Family was written with the goal of nurturing the spirit of family ('ohana), using the outrigger paddling community as its focus. We hope it will inspire young readers to appreciate the connective spirit of family and the shared companionship in this growing sport.

This book was inspired by Joey Alvarez of ARE Outrigger World and the film, *Family of the Wa'a*. Gratitude to Jackie Ovadia for creative/story input; Jeff Turcotte, Kay Parker, Marian Mejia, Noell Feesago, Chris Villaflor, and Joylynn Paman for editorial assistance; Sarah Clarehart for production assistance; and Michael Roney for project management and publishing through Highpoint Life Books.

A special thanks to Kimokeo Kapahulehua, of Maui, Hawai'i, without whom there would be no story; Billy Whitford, of Newport Aquatic Center (Newport Beach, CA) and the other directors of outrigger canoe clubs everywhere who have helped the sport of outrigger canoeing grow.

A portion of the proceeds from this book will go to the Kimokeo Foundation, which is privileged to spread the Hawai'ian cultural legacy, so it lasts for generations. The foundation partners with Maui's Hawai'ian immersion schools, helping secure school sites and providing educational support. Their belief: "If we don't preserve our native language, how will our culture survive?"

This is a story about family—or 'ohana (pronounced o-ha'-nah) as it is called in the Hawai'ian language. 'Ohana can include one's own family, close friends, or others who share a common interest. It is about a special kind of family—the family of outrigger paddlers—and a native Hawai'ian named Kimokeo (pronounced kee-mo-kay'-oh) who would grow up to spread the spirit of 'ohana.

As a boy, Kimokeo spent most of his days on the white-sand beaches of Hawai'i. He felt at home in the ocean and wasn't afraid of anything—not even the roughest waves.

Kimokeo was the biggest kid on the beach. Because of his size, the other kids looked up to him. He was untamed, free and wild, always looking for challenges.

At age 12, he found this challenge in outrigger paddling, where he could glide smoothly and effortlessly through the water.

It helped him feel at one
with the ocean.

One of his heroes was the the Hawai'ian god, Kanaloa, ruler of the seas. Kimokeo admired his power. He never imagined

that one day he, too, might become a hero to many boys and girls, in real life—a hero on water and on land.

One of Kimokeo's favorite stories was the one his parents often told him, about the 2,600-mile journey his ancestors took, hundreds of years ago. This was in wooden canoes, from Tahiti to Hawai'i. It inspired him to want to paddle even more and to find even bigger challenges.

At age 14, Kimokeo found this challenge and took paddling to the next level—the sport of outrigger racing. He entered his first race. Because he was so big and strong for his age, he did very well.

In the years that followed...

... he won many races.

But Kimokeo wasn't satisfied with just winning races. He wanted to share that feeling with others. In the spirit of 'ohana, he channeled his energy into teaching and inspiring others, nurturing the "family of the wa'a" (pronounced va'-ah)—the Tahitian word for outrigger.

In addition to winning many races, Kimokeo won the hearts of many people through his teaching. Out of respect, they called him "Uncle."

Uncle Kimokeo inspired many people to become paddlers and to teach their children how to paddle. That's how families grow.

He also trained and encouraged many teams of outrigger racers to push their limits and overcome the challenges of the waves and the wind on the open seas.

But his work was not complete.
One day, four visitors came to
his home: A 14-year-old boy, a
10-year-old girl, a young man
with a physical disability, and
a grownup cancer
survivor. They all
shared the dream
of paddling and hoped
Kimokeo could
help them.

Kimokeo taught the boy and the girl how to paddle. He even set up training camps to help many boys and girls discover the joys of outrigger paddling and racing, including children from inland areas where there were few opportunities to paddle.

Kimokeo helped them imagine the other awesome
"families" they might meet on the open waters.
Yes, dolphins and whales have families, too.

One of Kimokeo's greatest joys was introducing the boy with physical limitations to paddling to help him feel better about himself—no different than anyone else.

Meanwhile, others across the ocean were also introducing special groups to outrigger paddling, including helping blind and visually impaired athletes see their potential.

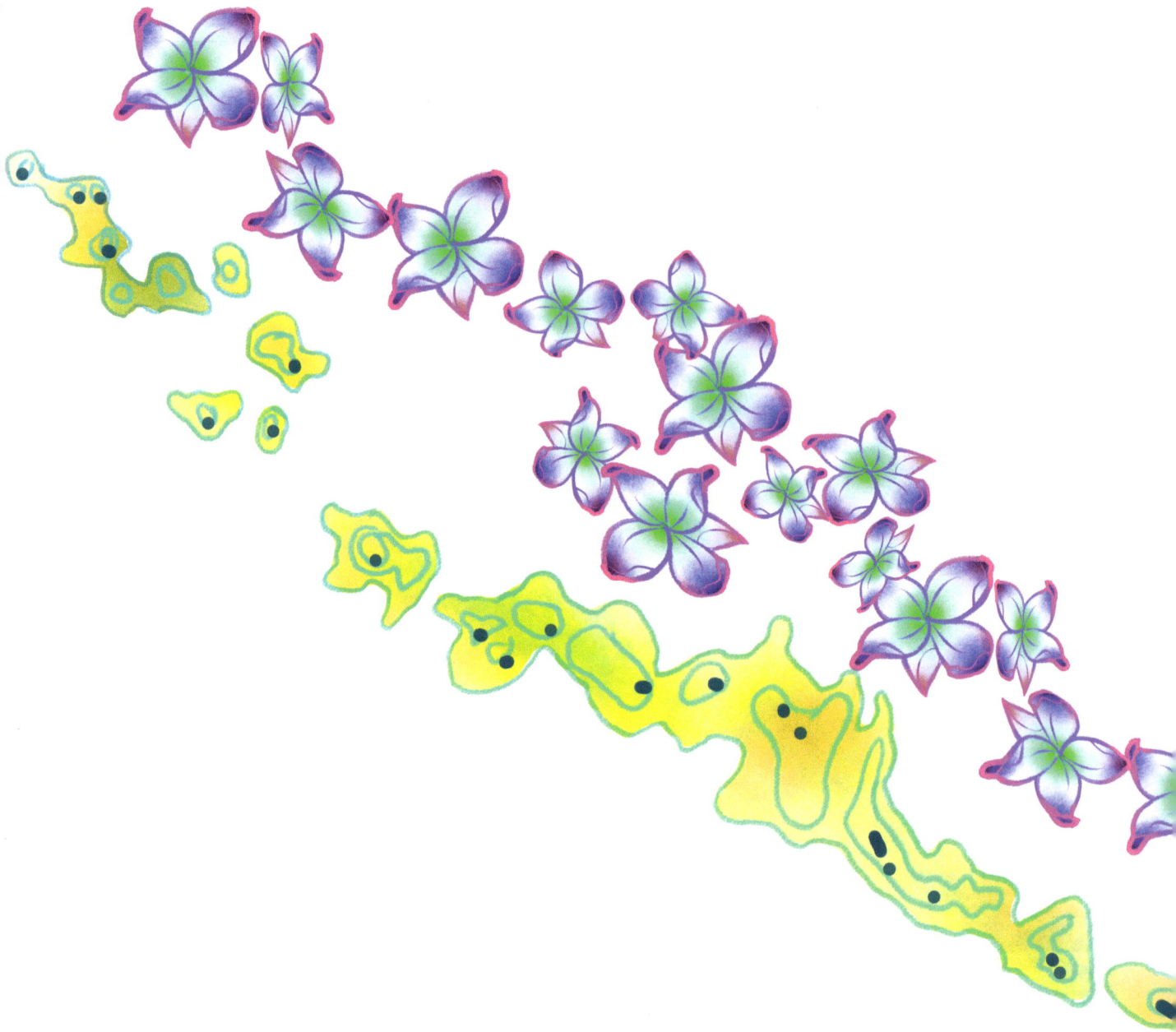

As for the cancer survivor, he was already an experienced paddler, so Kimokeo had a special challenge for him—being part of his 6-seat racing outrigger that would soon undertake an amazing journey.

It was a 400-mile voyage across open ocean waters connecting all the Hawai'ian Islands like a "flower lei."

This voyage wasn't a race, but for this man it was a race against time and the fear that his cancer might return.

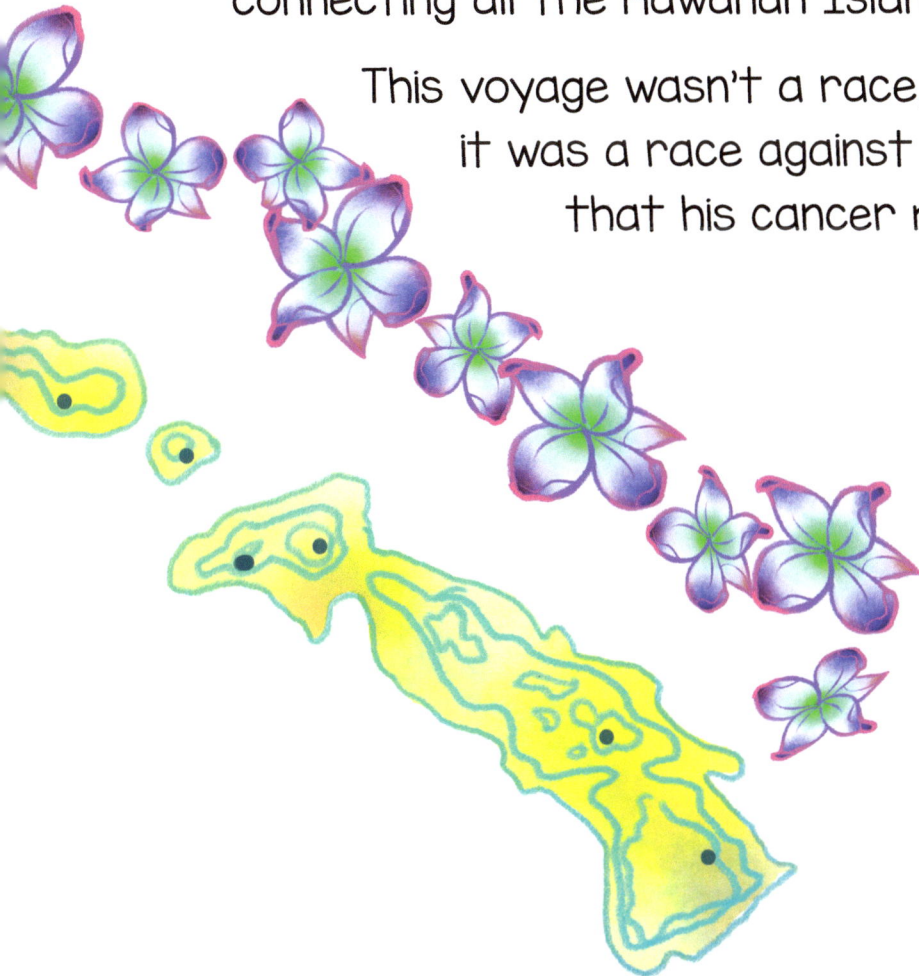

A "flower lei" is a string of flowers Hawai'ians sometimes wear around their necks when they greet people.

Then Kimokeo had an inspiration, and he discovered an even greater purpose in his life. After helping others achieve their goals and helping the sport of outrigger canoeing grow, Kimokeo himself needed to grow—to extend his influence beyond the water. Sometimes the teacher must become the student.

Kimokeo learned from a master teacher who taught him important lessons about Hawai'ian culture—and how the land, the sea, the heavens, and the people were all connected.

Now Kimokeo wanted to help others become more connected to the land, so they could take care of its precious resources.

He inspired young people to preserve and spread the Hawai'ian language and culture while encouraging the spirit of 'ohana in their community.

Already a larger-than-life figure, Kimokeo never stopped growing.

Today, Kimokeo still lives in Hawai'i. He has become a guiding light, spreading the spirit of 'ohana across the seas to faraway lands.

That same spirit of family has helped create many outrigger canoe clubs throughout the United States and around the world—in more than 75 countries. And the sport of outrigger canoeing continues to grow.

Paddlers can be found
wherever there is water—
on lakes and rivers, in
harbors, and in the ocean.

That's the power of 'ohana.
It helps bring many people
together, in a place where
they feel safe, at home,
and get a lot of support.

That's what a family is all about, where you feel a true sense of belonging—whether it's your own family, a family of friends, or a special kind of family—like the "family of the wa'a."

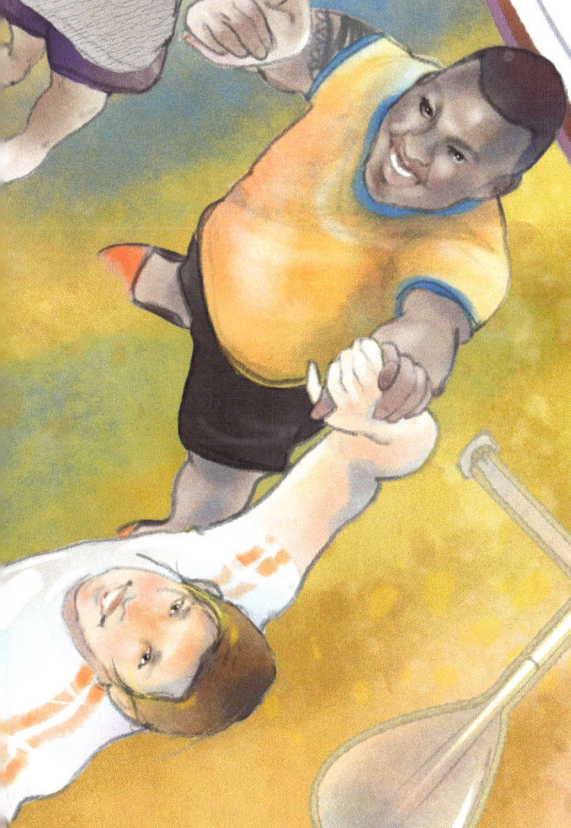

For more information on outrigger canoeing, please contact ARE Outrigger World at info@aretahiti.com.

www.ingramcontent.com/pod-product-compliance
Lightning Source LLC
Chambersburg PA
CBHW041542260326
41914CB00015B/1524